For Dylan
A.S.

To my family, for their love and support.
And much gratitude to Susan Pearson
for her insightful combination of Alice Schertle and myself.
Thanks also to Melanie Donovan, Rachel Simon, and Jerry Anton
for a wonderful working experience.
N.G.

LOTHROP, LEE & SHEPARD BOOKS   NEW YORK

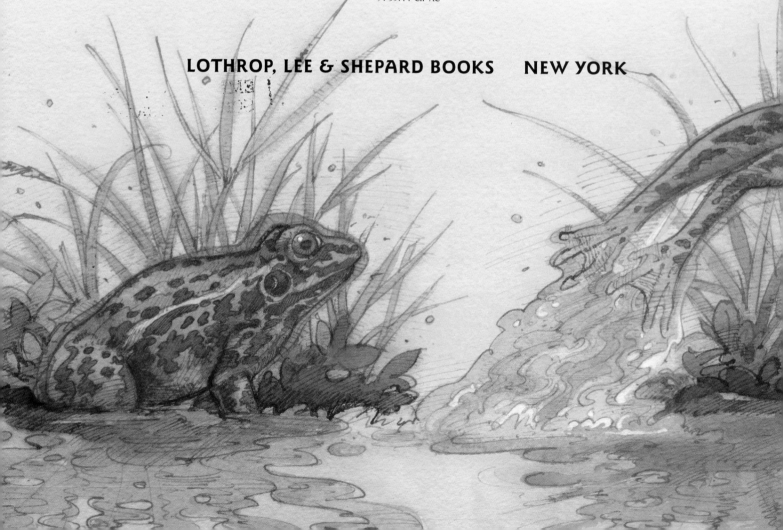

ALICE SCHERTLE & NORMAN GREEN

advice for a frog

Toucans

Picking fruit
isn't all
they're good for,
those boat beaks,
those blue and yellow
banana bills,
those pink and purple
splattered spatulas.

I have
seen you
ripping strips
of rainbow,
watched you
dragging the bright ribbons
through the branches
of the jungle trees.

Fruit Bats

All night
they flit among
the swollen globes, lancing
the tender skins and sucking sweet
juices . . . .

At dawn,
wrapped in their soft
leather leaves, they hang from
the branches in melon-bellied
bunches.

Pangolin

Ants are always busy:
bearing burdens larger
than themselves,
grading the ground,
moving their portion of planet
crumb by crumb.

When he comes
crashing into the mound
to run his sticky tongue
along their tunnels,
they cannot spare
more than a moment
for panic.

Even as he lumbers
from their walls,
ants are busy on repairs:
digging deeper channels,
building larger chambers,
excavating halls.

Or, mingling with his juices,
they liquefy, congeal,
adding strength to muscle,
welding, scale by scale,
impenetrable armor
to fortify his skin:
busy building,
cell by cell,
a bigger
pangolin.

Advice for a Frog
(Concerning a Crane)

Watch out, Old Croaker.
Here comes Stick Walker,
here comes Pond Poker,
here comes Death.

Take a breath, Slick Skin.
Muck down, sink in.
Don't make bubbles.
Good luck, Grin Chin—

here comes Trouble.

Frilled Lizard

Expansion Collar
Instructions for Operation

When not in use, the collar hangs in compact folds of skin conveniently tucked away beneath the wearer's chin.

Activate the collar by inflation of the lungs, full extension of the jaws, projection of the tongue.

Discourages a predator two times out of three. Batteries are not required.

Lifetime guarantee.

Harpy
Eagle

Hunger's keen eye slits the green
canopy, flashes down leafy
corridors, glints in dark
chambers, fastens
on a small
warm

m
e
a
l

Cheetah: The Race

Concentration
is essential:
Focus on the finish.
Dig your toes in,
leap off the line
and go for it!
No prize
for second place.
Grab victory
by the throat
and bring it down.

A Traveler's Tale

At dusk I ran along a mooring line
And slipped into the hold. That night I found
A berth behind a cask of Spanish wine.
We headed west to prove the earth was round.

There was another traveler of my kind
Who climbed aboard along the anchor chain.
On hardtack, meal and moldy bread we dined.
Our young were born upon the ship from Spain.

At length we found a land of mud and flowers.
I ran along the mooring line again
And slipped into the New World that was ours
And thanked the God who made both rats and men.

Galápagos Tortoise

I saw them come, the long canoes,
    the wanderers, the worshipers;
I saw the canvas sails appear,
    the mariners, discoverers;
I saw them bearing treasure chests,
    the castaways, the murderers;
I saw them come with instruments,
    the scientists, the measurers.
They leave their footprints on this ancient land.
I leave the future buried in the sand.

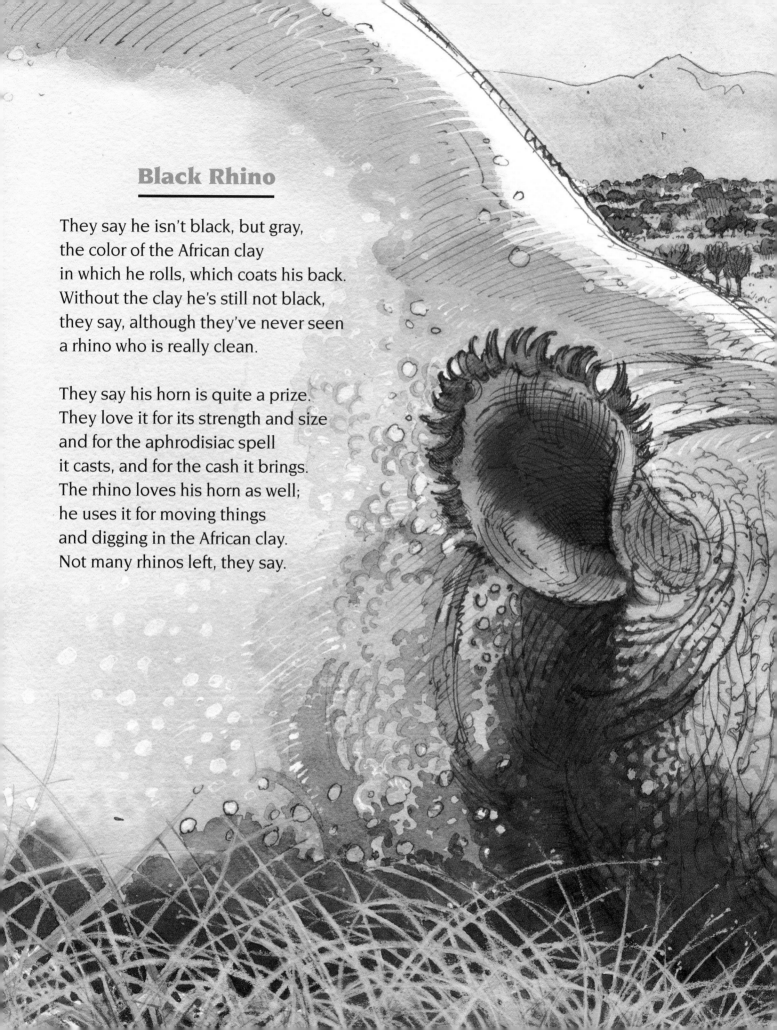

Black Rhino

They say he isn't black, but gray,
the color of the African clay
in which he rolls, which coats his back.
Without the clay he's still not black,
they say, although they've never seen
a rhino who is really clean.

They say his horn is quite a prize.
They love it for its strength and size
and for the aphrodisiac spell
it casts, and for the cash it brings.
The rhino loves his horn as well;
he uses it for moving things
and digging in the African clay.
Not many rhinos left, they say.

Again,
he keeps his vigil
on broad black wings,
watching from above the bloody
business, drawing his slow shadow
like a shroud across the scene.

Later,
he hunches on the plain.
His bald head bowed with grief,
he stays until the
smooth white bones
are clean.

Iguana

O, for the breath of flame
once more!
For wings that climbed
the spires of the skies
when heroes came
against me for the prize
and I was in my prime.
The world was different,
once upon a time.

Once more to hold
within my smoldering coils
the gleaming gold,
my hoard,
a dragon's spoils . . .
The ring that glittered
colder than a star,
the sheen of armor
that the hero wore,
the clinking coins,
the green and crimson stones
that winked at me
among the heroes' bones . . .

It was a different world, before.
O, for the breath of flame
once more!

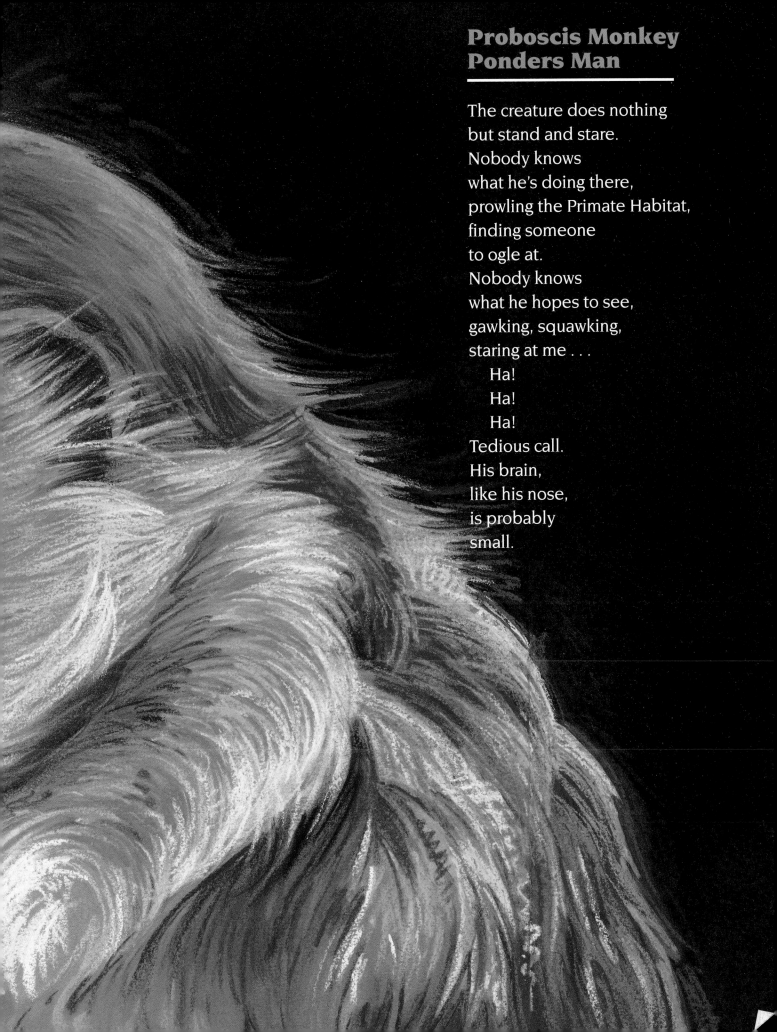

Proboscis Monkey
Ponders Man

The creature does nothing
but stand and stare.
Nobody knows
what he's doing there,
prowling the Primate Habitat,
finding someone
to ogle at.
Nobody knows
what he hopes to see,
gawking, squawking,
staring at me . . .
   Ha!
   Ha!
   Ha!
Tedious call.
His brain,
like his nose,
is probably
small.

Secretary Bird

Take a letter:

Say that
the ancient trees are falling.
Say that
the whale's song grows faint.
Say the passenger pigeon is gone.
The great auk is gone.
The rhino, the mountain gorilla,
almost gone . . .

Dip your quill
in the sludge
along the river,
in the soot
from the smokestack,
in the poisoned lake,
in the burning rain.
Dip it in the blood of the great blue whale.

Take a letter, bird:

to whom it may
concern

ABOUT THE ANIMALS IN THIS BOOK

Toucans: These relatives of the woodpecker live in the treetops of rain forests throughout South America, Central America, and Mexico. Flitting among the branches, toucans create dazzling flashes of color high in the jungle canopy. Their huge multicolored beaks look heavy, but are actually quite light and used primarily for picking fruit or cutting it into bite-size chunks.

Fruit Bats: Fruit bats roost in forests and swamps all over the world. The large bats illustrated here, sometimes called flying foxes, inhabit wooded areas of Southeast Asia, Australia, and the Pacific Islands. These flying mammals suck the juice and sometimes eat the pulp from fruit. Most species of flying foxes are endangered. Some are already extinct.

Pangolin: Sometimes called scaly anteaters, pangolins live in the woods and grasslands of Asia and Africa. They have no teeth but use their long, strong, sticky tongues to catch termites and ants. They can roll themselves into tight armored balls that predators cannot penetrate. Pangolins are hunted for their meat and for their scales, which some people believe have medicinal value. African pangolins, such as this one, are endangered.

Advice for a Frog (Crowned Crane): This handsome bird can be found along the edges of rivers and marshes in sub-Saharan Africa. Admired for its beauty, it is particularly valued because of its appetite for destructive pests, such as locusts. Crowned cranes also relish certain small animals, such as the frog illustrated here. In many cultures, the crane is a symbol of love and longevity because it often mates for life. The crowned crane is the national emblem of Uganda.

Frilled Lizard: This tough little lizard inhabits the woodlands of Australia and New Guinea. Although it lives mostly in trees, the frilled lizard can run swiftly on its hind legs for short distances. When the lizard is frightened, it extends the brightly colored collar of skin around its neck in order to appear more than a mouthful to predators.

Harpy Eagle: The most powerful of all the eagles lives in tall trees along rivers and in the mountain forests of southern Mexico and northeastern South America. Harpy eagles prey on monkeys, sloths, opossums, birds, and other tree-dwelling animals. The harpy's keen eyesight, far sharper than a human's, enables it to spot the slightest movement below as it soars high above the trees. The continued existence of this regal bird is threatened by destruction of the rain forests.

Cheetah: The Race: The fastest animal in the world, this graceful cat can reach speeds of seventy miles per hour over short distances. For thousands of years, humans tamed and trained cheetahs as hunting animals. Now the large cats are often killed for their beautiful spotted fur and to prevent them from attacking cattle. Although the cheetah once flourished throughout Africa, India, and Asia, it has completely disappeared in Asia and is endangered in Africa.

A Traveler's Tale (Brown Rat): Also called the Norway rat, this rodent is thought to have originated in China and spread with humans all over the world. Rats are one of the most populous mammal groups on earth. Like humans, they are omnivorous and can eat practically anything. By nature woodland creatures, they adapt easily to living near people.

Galápagos Tortoise: *Galápago* is the Spanish word for "tortoise." These huge land turtles are found only on the islands that bear their name. When humans discovered the Galápagos Islands off the coast of South America, they slaughtered thousands of tortoises for their shells and meat. Although now protected by law, these slow-moving giants are endangered. A Galápagos tortoise that survives the perils of today's world may live to be well over one hundred years old.

Black Rhino: This huge beast, which once flourished in the scrub of eastern and southern Africa, is now on the edge of extinction. The rhinoceros is often slaughtered for its horn, which in some cultures is thought to have medicinal value or power as a love potion. In 1980, there were over three thousand rhinos in the Central African Republic. All have been killed by poachers. Poaching accounts for the deaths of ninety percent of all adult black rhinos.

The Mourner (King Vulture): A close relative of the California condor, the king vulture inhabits the tropical forests of Mexico and Central and South America. On great dark wings, it circles above sick or injured animals, waiting for death to come. Scientists think this carrion eater may be one of the few birds to locate its food by sense of smell. Like the harpy eagle's, the king vulture's existence depends on the ever-shrinking rain forests.

Iguana: The common iguana lives along forest rivers in Mexico and Central and South America. It is an excellent swimmer and climber. This large lizard can grow to be more than six feet long, and its powerful tail is a formidable weapon. Iguanas are beginning to appear in the wild in the United States, perhaps because people buy young iguanas as pets and abandon them when they begin to grow.

Proboscis Monkey Ponders Man: Only older male proboscis monkeys sport the long, pendulous noses that give this species its name. These monkeys, the best swimmers among the primates, are found on the island of Borneo. As the mangrove swamps they inhabit have been destroyed by developers, the number of monkeys has dwindled. They are now endangered.

Secretary Bird: Common in Africa south of the Sahara, this bird of prey hunts snakes, birds, insects, and small mammals. Flying only when absolutely necessary, it prefers to run swiftly across the grasslands on its long legs. The secretary bird got its name from the unusual crest of feathers on its head. Some people thought the long feathers looked like the quill pens secretaries used to stick behind their ears.